INTO Wild Africa

BLACKBIRCH®
PRESS

THOMSON
™
GALE

San Diego • Detroit • New York • San Francisco • Cleveland • New Haven, Conn. • Waterville, Maine • London • Munich

© 2004 by Blackbirch Press™. Blackbirch Press™ is an imprint of The Gale Group, Inc., a division of Thomson Learning, Inc.

Blackbirch Press™ and Thomson Learning™ are trademarks used herein under license.

For more information, contact
The Gale Group, Inc.
27500 Drake Rd.
Farmington Hills, MI 48331-3535
Or you can visit our Internet site at http://www.gale.com

LIBRARY OF CONGRESS CATALOGING-IN-PUBLICATION DATA

Into wild Africa / Elaine Pascoe, book editor.
    p. cm. — (The Jeff Corwin experience)
Based on an episode from a Discovery Channel program hosted by Jeff Corwin.
Summary: Television personality Jeff Corwin takes the reader on an expedition to Africa to learn about the diverse wildlife found there.
Includes index.
  ISBN 1-56711-851-8 (alk. paper) — ISBN 1-4103-0172-9 (pbk. : alk. paper)
  1. Africa —Description and travel—Juvenile literature. 2. Natural areas— Africa —Juvenile literature. 3. Wilderness areas— Africa —Juvenile literature. 4. Corwin, Jeff—Journeys— Africa —Juvenile literature. [1. Zoology— Africa. 2. Africa —Description and travel. 3. Corwin, Jeff.] I. Pascoe, Elaine. II. Corwin, Jeff. III. Series.
  DT1536.I57 2004
  916.881—dc21   2003009278

Printed in China
10 9 8 7 6 5 4 3 2 1

Ever since I was a kid, I dreamed about traveling around the world, visiting exotic places, and seeing all kinds of incredible animals. And now, guess what? That's exactly what I get to do!

Yes, I am incredibly lucky. But, you don't have to have your own television show on Animal Planet to go off and explore the natural world around you. I mean, I travel to Madagascar and the Amazon and all kinds of really cool places—but I don't need to go that far to see amazing wildlife up close. In fact, I can find thousands of incredible critters right here, in my own backyard—or in my neighbor's yard (he does get kind of upset when he finds me crawling around in the bushes, though). The point is, no matter where you are, there's fantastic stuff to see in nature. All you have to do is look.

I love snakes, for example. Now, I've come face to face with the world's most venomous vipers—some of the biggest, some of the strongest, and some of the rarest. But I've also found an amazing variety of snakes just traveling around my home state of Massachusetts. And I've taken trips to preserves, and state parks, and national parks—and in each place I've enjoyed unique and exciting plants and animals. So, if I can do it, you can do it, too (except for the hunting venomous snakes part!). So, plan a nature hike with some friends. Organize some projects with your science teacher at school. Ask mom and dad to put a state or a national park on the list of things to do on your next family vacation. Build a bird house. Whatever. But get out there.

As you read through these pages and look at the photos, you'll probably see how jazzed I get when I come face to face with beautiful animals. That's good. I want you to feel that excitement. And I want you to remember that—even if you don't have your own TV show—you can still experience the awesome beauty of nature almost anywhere you go—any day of the week. I only hope that I can help bring that awesome power and beauty a little closer to you. Enjoy!

Best Wishes!
Jeff

INTO
Wild Africa

It's the Africa you've never imagined—
home of the oldest desert on earth...
the fastest land mammal...the quickest
serpent. I want to show you a harsh
and beautiful land known as Namibia.
Namibia's desert, bush, and grasslands
create a great palette of discovery,
filled with creatures for us to find.

I'm Jeff Corwin.
Welcome to Africa.

Namibia has a harsh environment.

AFRICA

Namibia

See why they call it a sidewinder?

Small, but very venomous.

Check this out. In my hands is a delicate but very venomous snake, a desert sidewinder. It's also called Peringuey's adder, but it's commonly known as a sidewinder because of the way it moves. It throws the top part of its body forward, and then the rest of the body follows in loops as it moves across the sand. Only a small part of the body touches the hot sand at one time.

This sidewinder looks diminutive and fragile, but he packs a potent bite. He is a viper and, as with most species of vipers, his venom is designed to both kill prey and destroy the tissue of the prey, to make the digestion process that much easier.

His body is brown almost to the very end, but the tip of his tail is black. He uses his tail as a lure. He twitches and dangles that lure, bringing in hungry lizards. Then he bites them, kills them with his venom, and swallows them whole.

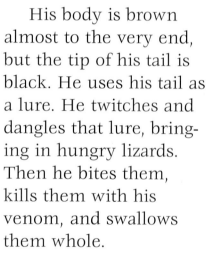

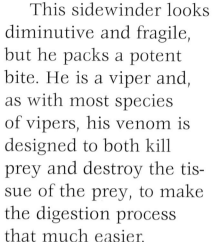

This snake is a beautiful creature, a wonderful introduction into the world we call Namibia.

Namibia's wilderness is home to the San people. They're masters of survival. They have carved out an existence in one of the toughest habitats on our planet.

Here I am with two of my San friends.

Survival here is all about finding water. The San know about one particular plant that, when dug up, reveals an enormous taproot. Once the root has been grated and mashed, it can serve as a lifesaving source of water.

This root has a high water content.

Tracking lessons

When it comes to tracking, these people are masters—and they have to be. For centuries, it was a matter of survival. They can find a tiny tortoise or a big warthog.

See the little flecks of black?

Look at this guy— a beautiful tortoise. This is the leopard tortoise. This specific individual is sort of faded, but if you look very closely at its carapace, its top shell, you'll see the little flecks of black that give it a leopardlike appearance. These are ancient reptiles that have been roaming the grasslands and bush veldt of Africa for millions and millions of years. You can tell he's a tortoise, as opposed to a water turtle, by the domelike appearance of that shell. Tortoises like this are primarily herbivores. They eat tender shoots and grasses, mushrooms, berries, and occasionally they'll eat insects.

As with most tortoises, this guy's most important defense is his shell. If a predator comes too close, he pulls himself in and actually creates a fortress. He brings his legs in, and he's got his own sort of castle doors to seal in all the delicious stuff that a honey badger some other predator would like to eat.

This is one desert survival specialist.

Next up: a game drive.

Wildebeest

Kudu

Mountain Zebra

To the northeast of the desert, Namibia offers up a dramatic big game experience. Oryx, wildebeest, and kudu can be found by exploring this wild countryside. We're just keeping our eyes out for wildlife.

Right here we have a small herd of mountain zebra. We have a colt, and we have some adults. There are some big differences between the mountain zebras and the plains zebras. The first thing you'll notice is that the chin of the mountain zebra has a dewlap, a flap of skin. And on the mountain zebra, the mane is a little thicker.

This monitor lizard is not happy to be held.

The bush veldt is not only a good place for spotting mammals, but also a place where you might find a member of the *varanidae* family—a monitor lizard—just meandering across the road. This fellow tells us with his deep, growl-like hiss that he's not happy to see us. He scuttles into an acacia tree, and when I go to get him I'm stuck at every angle by the tree's thorns—but the lizard is beautiful.

These lizards have excellent vision.

This is the savanna monitor, and his name tells you where he loves to live—in the bush veldt and grasslands of central and southern Africa. He's a very good-sized lizard, definitely adult, pushing 4 feet in length. What I love about monitors is they're very snake-like. In fact, if you look in this lizard's mouth, you'll see that his tongue is forked like a snake's. Also like snakes, he's got an extraordinary sense of taste— he tastes his way through the world. He also has a good sense of smell, excellent vision, pretty good hearing, and sharp teeth. And like a snake, when this creature grabs onto prey, he swallows it whole. He'll eat everything from lizards, snakes, birds, and birds' eggs, to small mammals— all sorts of creatures, dead and alive.

A forked tongue helps the monitor to smell.

This predator is very snakelike.

Giraffes are an incredible part of the African landscape.

Like finding lizards, finding giraffes is easy here. But getting close to them—well, that's another story. Sometimes you'll spot a pair of them, but usually they're found in herds of twelve to fifteen. Amazingly, a giraffe can go more than a month without drinking water. The giraffe has a well-developed sense of smell, hearing, and vision. Research has indicated that they may even communicate with each other with infrasonic sounds.

These guys see me...

So much for being stealthy.

I'm thinking I'll hide under the branches and be really stealthy and sneak up close to this giraffe. But the giraffe sees me and says, "Look at that person down there—he thinks he's hiding. But you're stupid, Jeff Corwin—bye."

Vultures perch high above the landscape.

In this hardscrabble environment practically everything is a life-sustaining source of food. Hyenas and jackals, as well as these vultures, are on the constant look out for carrion—which is dead meat.

This giraffe has died. And I can see a wound by its hoof region that suggests maybe it was bitten by a snake. If it was the bite of a black mamba that brought this animal down, then that's all the more reason for us to be cautious. But there's a great story here. This creature is now being incorporated back into the ecosystem. Whether he wants to or not, he's part of the life cycle for other creatures, like vultures.

This giraffe is now part of the food supply for other creatures.

Vultures led me to the dead giraffe, but I won't have any help finding elephants in this part of Namibia. There's only one small herd occupying this area of more than 50,000 acres—but perhaps the African gods are smiling on us today. I can hear a herd of elephants. We're just going to wait right here and see if they'll move toward us.

Vultures are part of nature's cleanup crew.

You don't miss these guys coming.

African elephants are the largest terrestrial mammals on our planet. Now, if your

Elephants like to stick together.

Not trampled... yet.

only experience with an African elephant comes from the circus or the zoo, you really have no idea how dangerous these creatures can be in the wild. They're very protective of each other. They act as a group, and at 3 tons each, this is one group you certainly don't want to mess with. This is their turf, and if you don't respect them, you're going to regret it. We need to be very careful and very quiet.

Crunching, crashing, the pushing of branches and debris, the disturbance in the forest—and then, appearing out of nowhere, five young elephants, fifteen-year-old elephants. From our perspective, they are huge. They keep coming and coming and coming and I'm thinking they're going to squish me. I'm so nervous all I can do is giggle, masking my fright with laughter.

At 3 tons, this is an African animal to be admired from afar.

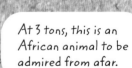

Looking for rhinos...

Central Namibia is home to southern Africa's most magnificent creatures, including the fabled white rhino. One of the best places to see them is the Ocheeva game reserve. Peter Reinhardt and his crew may be able to get me close to one of these legendary giants. Our chief tracker, Marius, carries an automatic weapon, not for hunting but for protection from poachers.

White rhinos are highly endangered.

Right off we spot a huge white rhino, a bull. He might weigh upwards of 4,000 pounds. A colossal creature, but he gets wind of us and takes off. So Peter takes us to another spot in Ocheeva, where rhinos are a little more approachable.

This guy is probably a 2500-pounder. He's checking me out. Now if he should charge us, we'll likely be OK as long as we stand still because white rhinos don't have very good vision. They're not good at picking out individual things in their environment. Basically, they react to movement. Their senses of smell and hearing are extremely strong, but the wind is working with us and blowing our smell away. If the wind was blowing our smell toward this creature, we would be in trouble. So I'm just going to stand still and relax. I'm not nervous.

You're probably thinking, "OK, Jeff, if he does charge and you have to run, no problem—you're a fit, good-looking guy who knows how to run, right?" I do like to run. But surprisingly, even though this creature weighs 2,500 pounds, he can roll into a 35-mile-an-hour gallop. I cannot run 35 miles an hour.

This guy can run about 35mph when he gets going.

Look at his ears. He's rotating those ears individually so he can pick up sound in a complete radius, 360 degrees. His hearing is extraordinary.

This is an orphan rhino.

Cute little gal...

For all its size and keen senses, the rhino continues to be victimized by poachers. It's a tragedy that results in countless orphans like this one, named Chica, who's being raised at Ocheeva. When they got her, she was only a tiny calf, a couple of months old. Peter said he could pick her up with both arms.

Here's a challenge: Look at this creature and try to figure out where it fits in the animal world. You might think it's related to a cow. But in fact, the rhino is more closely related to a horse. Tapirs, horses, and rhinos belong to the perissodactyl group.

Elke and Chica are bonding.

24 liters per day

Chica is lovingly cared for by Peter and his wife, Elke. It will still be a few months before she's weaned off the milk bottle. She drinks 24 liters of milk a day, and they feed her a horse supplement. Since she belongs to the horse group, it works just fine for her.

One of the creatures we came to find here, the black mamba, inhabits a wide variety of terrain. Now, these snakes are not rare, but they never seem to be around when you're looking for them. As the sun comes out, snakes for the most part take shelter under what little shade they can find in these little tufts of scrappy vegetation.

Here's a nice area for a snake. It has the shade of the trees and a hole in there. I'm just going to probe and see if I can feel anything moving...

The black mamba is an awesome snake. Highly venomous.

Puff adders are quite dangerous.

Look at this—is this not beautiful or what? This is a puff adder. They call him a puff adder because when he's agitated, he'll coil

He's a little agitated...

up and send out a raspy hiss. Now, although he's not a black mamba, he is extremely venomous. But his venom is different from that of a black mamba. This creature produces a hemo- or cytotoxin, while the black mamba produces a neurotoxin.

Notice how I keep my distance...

These guys are not to be messed with.

Although the black mamba is easily the most venomous snake, the puff adder accounts for 60 percent of the serious snakebites that people acquire in Africa. The reason is that puff adders so brilliantly blend in with the surrounding real estate that people don't see them. You could easily step into this bush and not know that underneath was a very cantankerous snake.

Getting to know a dwarf chameleon.

He's trying to scare me.

Here's a really, really cool creature—a dwarf chameleon. Right now, he's bluffing, making himself look larger. He's opening his mouth, he's stretching his jaw, and he's doubling his size. He wants you to think he's too big for you to swallow.

These are extraordinary lizards. His ability to blend in so precisely with the environment around him is the result of little packets of pigments that are scattered throughout his skin. They're called chromatophores. The packets can dilate and constrict, and that process creates different shades of color.

Look at him blend in...

Two eyes out...

Now, one looking back at me!

Look at his face. Each eye moves individually. For example, he could have one eye looking at you while at the same time keeping an eye on me. Or he can bring both eyes together and have a really good sense of the depth in front of him.

Let's set this guy back and continue on.

Central Namibia is home to a number of conservation projects. This one, called Africat, works with some of Africa's most threatened and wild residents, cheetahs and leopards.

This older female leopard was caught hunting livestock on a nearby farm. Lucky for her, the farmer who trapped her decided to bring her to Africat instead of shooting her. While she's here, Lucky will be rehydrated and her blood will be collected. That way, Africat has a permanent record of her genetic history. After going through a comprehensive medical exam, she will be released on Africat property, spending the rest of her life on more than 35,000 acres of protected bush veldt.

African leopard

Africat has a large tract of protected land.

See the camouflage at work?

Let your eyes just scan this landscape quickly, and you don't see anything. But buried within this horizon of grass are very powerful, amazing carnivores. And there's more than one of them. They're cheetahs. And this is a wonderful illustration of how these creatures can almost magically disappear into their habitat. They have beautiful camouflage—black spots all

These are incredibly beautiful creatures.

The spots confuse the eye.

The world's fastest land animal...

over their bodies that break up the shape and uniformity of an individual animal.

Cheetahs are built for speed. I like to think of them as the Lamborghinis or the Porsches of African cats. Their heads lie low to the ground, their backs are slightly arched, their feet stretch out like running shoes. And then—swoosh, they take off at speeds of up to 60 miles an hour to take down their prey.

Saying "hi" to Lori.

This is an important destination for our journey in Namibia. It's the Cheetah Conservation Fund (CCF). We're with Lori, the director, and we're going to help work on a cheetah. This nine-year-old cheetah was trapped by a rancher and it spent a number of days in a cage in 100-degree-plus weather. It is now severely dehydrated and has an injured paw.

This poor guy was injured.

In addition to rescuing injured cheetahs, CCF has a conservation program designed to educate local villagers, ranchers, and even school children. Ultimately, the mission of the Cheetah Conservation Fund is to maintain the population of wild cheetahs through rehabilitation, outreach, and education.

This is Chabacca.

Chabacca, CCF's official ambassador, was orphaned at three weeks and hand raised by Lori. He's used in educational programs at the center. See what he's doing? He smells something on this old, twisted tree. To us this is just a piece of wood, but to this great cat it's his play tree. Trees like this are extremely important to cheetahs in this part of the world. He's smelling the signatures that he has left behind in his urine, and maybe the signatures of other cheetahs that passed through, challenging his territory. And here where the grass is high, the trees give these animals a place to check out the landscape and look for prey.

It's a seal beach!

On Namibia's west coast, where this parched land meets the south Atlantic Ocean, is Cape Cross. It is home to a colony of animals you might not expect to find in Africa. Here you'll see thousands of Cape fur seals gathered in a terrific colony. This region contains more than one hundred thousand of these amazing pinnipeds. Although they're called Cape fur seals, they have the flappy ears, flippers, and body design of sea lions.

They look like sea lions but they're seals.

The males, or bulls, are much larger than the females. Males are about 8 feet in length and near 500 pounds in weight. But, if you look around here, you won't see any seals that are 8 feet in length. Most are around 5 feet in length and weigh about 200 to 300 pounds. Why? Because all the males are gone. They came here, did their business, made their families, and left these females behind to nurture their offspring.

These pups are so cute.

The adorable, furry pups are all about one and a half to two months in age. These pups are dependent upon their mothers for milk up into the age of four to five months. It's at that point that they begin to shift from drinking mother's milk to partaking of what the sea can offer—things like mollusks, crustaceans, and fish.

Each one of the females claims a bit of shore, an individual rock, as her territory. She acts like this is a chunk of Beverly Hills. And she defends that rock with barks, nips, bites, and slaps of her flippers.

Each female claims a territory.

I'm learning a very interesting lesson from these African fur seals, and that lesson is that life is as tough along this coastline as it is in that harsh desert behind you. And nowhere is that more evident than on this particular tract of beach. It's all been packed tightly

Lots of seals, little space.

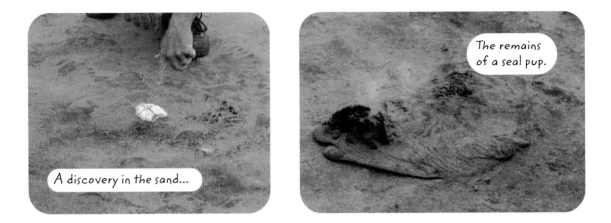

A discovery in the sand...

The remains of a seal pup.

down from the weight of heavy seals, and mixed with this earth are some very interesting rocks. Check them out—they're very white, almost like ivory. Look closely. What appears to be some sort of white rock is actually the skull, the remains of a seal pup. And the hard reality for these creatures is that one out of four of these pups will die within the first few months of their lives. There are a number of reasons why these creatures die off at such a rapid rate. They can be separated from their mothers, and when that happens they starve to death. They can even be crushed by an adult seal that's not paying attention to where it's moving. All these factors add up and make the odds of survival very low for these creatures.

Now it's time to move back into mamba mode. I'm headed for the area where we are going to find another one of these great long black serpents.

The black mamba is one of the most dangerous snakes in the world, and I am in seventh heaven right now. For a herpetologist to see this creature face to face—it doesn't get any better than this. When you first think of the mamba, you think dangerous, cruel, ornery, and ugly. But it's a spectacular creature when respected, and one that really brings home the beauty and the magnificence of Africa. Mambas can reach to about 12 or 14 feet in length. That's a huge animal.

These are large dangerous animals.

His fangs only come out when he's ready to bite.

This snake isn't trying to escape, it's holding its ground. That is one of the reasons why people here fear the black mamba. The snake is lightning fast—his strike is nothing but a blur. He's a member of the elapid snake family. And he's a little different because he has control over his fangs. They lie back along his jaw, and then spring forward when he's ready to bite.

I have to be very careful here.

I have to really watch what I'm doing. I can't get lost

in conversation, because before you know it, this snake will sneak about two inches out of my grasp and then, boom, land me with a very powerful bite. Then I'd be in trouble, serious trouble, because the venom in this snake is potent. It is a neurotoxin, a venom that's designed to shut down the nervous system of his prey, so he can immobilize and kill it. If this mamba were to land a bite on me, I would have anywhere from a half an hour to four hours to start receiving antivenin. If you're bitten by this snake, and you don't get the antivenin, you are going to die.

This guy's bite is a serious weapon.

Is Namibia cool, or what?

I can't speak for you, but for myself, I'm thrilled and honored to be so close to a wonderful creature like the black mamba. On our journey to Namibia, not only did we encounter the fastest cat on our planet, the cheetah, we also got to experience and discover the world's fastest snake. It's a great way for us to end our adventure, so I'm going to very carefully unwrap this guy. There he goes.

I wasn't bitten, so it looks like we have a lot more wildlife and exploration experiences ahead. I'll see you on our next adventure.

Glossary

antivenin the antidote for a snake's venom

carapace the top part of a turtle's shell

carnivores animals that eat meat

carrion the remains of a dead animal

conservation preservation or protection

crustacean a type of aquatic animal such as a shrimp, crab, or lobster

cytotoxin a poison that damages cells

dewlap a flap of skin

elapid a type of venomous snake

habitat a place where animals and plants live naturally together

herbivores animals that eat plants

herpetologist a scientist who study reptiles and amphibians

infrasonic a sound frequency below the range of the human ear

mammal a warm-blooded animal that feeds its babies with milk

mollusk a type of animal that includes snails, clams, and octopi

neurotoxin venom that damages the nervous system

poachers people who illegally kill or capture wild animals

predator an animal that kills and eats other animals

rehabilitation healing and restoring strength

reptiles cold-blooded, usually egg-laying animals such as snakes and lizards

serpent snake

terrestrial of or on the earth

venom a poison used by snakes to attack their prey or defend themselves

venomous having a gland that produces poison for self-defense or hunting

viper a type of venomous snake

Index

FRIDA KAHLO

Famous Mexican Artist

Mateo Alvarez

E **Enslow Publishing**
101 W. 23rd Street
Suite 240
New York, NY 10011
USA

enslow.com

Words to Know

canvas—A strong cloth on which artists often paint.

divorce—To end a marriage.

gallery—A room or building where art is shown.

mural—A huge painting on the walls of a building.

photographer—A person who takes pictures with a camera.

polio—A disease that attacks the muscles and makes it hard to walk. The disease is very rare today.

self-portrait—An artist's picture of himself or herself.

trolley—A streetcar that runs on tracks.

Contents

Frida Kahlo

CHAPTER 1

Growing Up

On July 6, 1907, Frida Kahlo was born in a house known as "La Casa Azul" (The Blue House). Her home was in a small Mexican village called Coyoacán. Frida's mother, Matilde Calderón, was very strict and serious. Frida was closer to her father, Guillermo. He worked as a **photographer** and taught Frida how to take pictures. Frida had three sisters: Matilde, Adriana, and Cristina.

When she was a young girl, Frida became very sick. To help her get better, her father encouraged her to play lots of sports.

When Frida was six years old, she became ill with **polio**, a serious disease. She had to stay in bed for nine months. She finally got better, but her right leg was smaller than the left one.

School Days

Frida's mother did not think girls needed to go to high school. But her father wanted her to get a good education. When Frida was fifteen, she passed the test to get into one of the top high schools in Mexico City. She hoped to be a doctor one day.

At school, Frida joined a group called "La Cachuchas" (The Caps). The students, who wore

Frida was born in this blue house (La Casa Azul) and spent much of her life here.

red caps, were very smart and enjoyed talking about books. But they also liked to have fun and play pranks. Once, they rode a donkey down the hallway of the school.

One day a famous artist named Diego Rivera came to the school. He began painting a **mural** on the school walls. Diego's murals showed the people and history of Mexico. Frida loved to watch Diego paint.

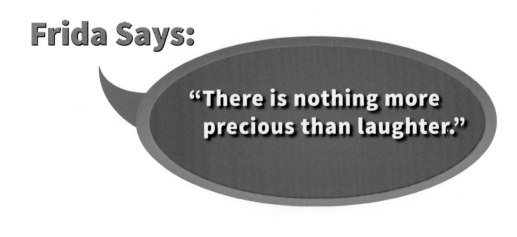

Frida Says:

"There is nothing more precious than laughter."

CHAPTER 2

The Accident

When Frida was eighteen years old, she was in an accident that changed her life forever. On September 17, 1925, she and a friend were on a bus on their way home from school. Suddenly a **trolley** car crashed into the bus. Some people were killed. A metal pole went through Frida's body and her back was broken in three places. Other bones were broken too. An ambulance rushed her to the hospital.

Frida was hurt so badly the doctors thought she would die. She spent a month in the hospital. From her neck to her hips, Frida was wrapped in a stiff cast. She could not move. After she went home, she still had to wear a cast and stay in bed for months.

Starting to Paint

To take her mind off her troubles, Frida began to paint. Her father brought brushes, paints,

Frida Says:

"Feet, what do I need you for when I have wings to fly?"

Frida painted while she was in the hospital. She liked drawing self-portraits, like the one shown here.

and **canvas** to her bedside. At first, she did portraits of her family and her friends. Looking in a mirror hanging over her bed, she painted **self-portraits**—that is, pictures of herself.

This photo was taken one year after Frida's accident.

After a few months, Frida could walk again. Her back would hurt for the rest of her life. But Frida was stronger and braver than the pain. Frida had another operation on her back in 1927. Again she was in a stiff cast. Again she showed her feelings with brushes and paint. Frida used art to express more than she could say in words.

CHAPTER 3

Life with Diego

Frida decided to show her art to Diego Rivera. He told her that she had talent and that she should keep painting. The two became friends and soon they fell in love. On August 21, 1929, Frida married Diego. She was twenty-one years old. He was forty-one.

Frida began to dress in traditional Mexican clothes because Diego liked them. After a while, she became well known for wearing colorful clothes, lots of big jewelry, and interesting hairstyles. Some people said Frida made herself look like a work of art.

Diego sometimes spent years painting a mural.

Diego's murals often showed the history of Mexico. This one is on the National Palace of Mexico City.

Going to America

Diego's murals were famous in the United States. He and Frida traveled to California, Michigan, and New York. They were very popular everywhere they went. Diego and Frida went to parties at the homes of rich and important people. But Frida was not happy.

Frida was homesick for her family, for the foods and places of Mexico. Diego loved the United States. He liked the factories and noise of the cities. To Frida, the United States was a dirty place. The rich people were too rich, and the poor people were too poor. Frida wanted to go home.

Frida got her wish. In 1933 she and Diego went back to Mexico.

Frida Says:

"I never paint dreams or nightmares. I paint my own reality."

CHAPTER 4

Frida's Fame

Back home, Frida picked up her paintbrushes again. She made small paintings on wood or canvas. Frida's artwork was very personal. It showed her feelings about her life. In all, Frida painted fifty-five self-portraits.

An art **gallery** in New York City put on a show of Frida's work in 1938, and she sold a painting. It was her first sale. The next year, she had a show in Paris, France. The Louvre, a famous art

Frida was the first Latina to be honored on a US stamp.

Frida often sat here in this wheelchair to paint in her studio.

museum, bought one of her self-portraits. Frida was becoming famous.

Final Years

Even though Frida and Diego loved each other, they had a difficult marriage. They often argued. In 1939 they **divorced**. But Frida and Diego hated being apart. They remarried the following year.

Frida began teaching at the School of Painting and Sculpture. Her students loved her. But her health was getting worse. Frida had been in pain

Frida Says:

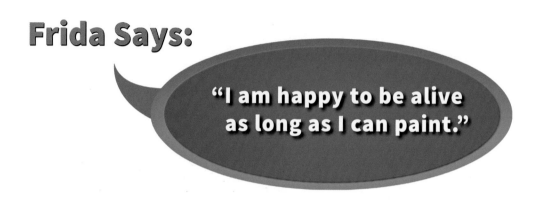

"I am happy to be alive as long as I can paint."

since her accident. When she could not travel to the school, she invited the students to her house.

In 1953 one of Frida's friends put together a special show to honor Frida and her work. Frida was in terrible pain, but she refused to stay home. Frida arrived by ambulance, dressed in her finest Mexican clothes and jewelry. The crowd went wild.

Frida died on July 13, 1954, in La Casa Azul, the house where she was born. It is now the Frida Kahlo Museum.

The Two Fridas is one of Frida's most famous paintings.

Frida Kahlo never painted to become rich or famous. Instead, she painted to show her feelings about herself and the world. The joy and the pain that she felt in her life can still be seen in her artwork today.

Timeline

1907—Frida Kahlo is born in Coyoacán, Mexico, on July 6.

1913—Frida becomes ill with polio.

1925—Frida is badly hurt in a bus accident. She begins to paint while lying in bed.

1929—Frida marries Diego Rivera on August 21.

1938—Frida has an art show in New York City.

1939—Frida's art is shown in Paris, France. Frida and Diego get a divorce.

1940—Frida and Diego marry again on December 8.

1943—Frida begins teaching art at the School of Painting and Sculpture in Mexico City.

1953—Frida has her only art show in Mexico.

1954—Frida dies in La Casa Azul on July 13.

Learn More

Books

Deuchars, Marion. *Draw Paint Print Like the Great Artists*. London: Laurence King, 2014.

Fabiny, Sarah. *Who Was Frida Kahlo?* New York: Grosset & Dunlap, 2013.

McManus, Lori. *Mexican Culture*. Chicago: Heinemann, 2012.

Rubin, Susan Goldman. *Diego Rivera: An Artist for the People*. New York: Harry N. Abrams, 2013.

Web Sites

pbs.org/weta/fridakahlo

"Life and Times of Frida Kahlo" has information, photographs, and pictures of Frida's art.

fridakahlo.org

Includes a biography, quotes, and pictures of Frida's paintings.

Index

Published in 2016 by Enslow Publishing, LLC.
101 W. 23rd Street, Suite 240, New York, NY 10011

Copyright © 2016 by Enslow Publishing, LLC.

All rights reserved.

No part of this book may be reproduced by any means without the written permission of the publisher.

Cataloging-in-Publication Data

Alvarez, Mateo.
Frida Kahlo: famous Mexican artist / by Mateo Alvarez.
p. cm.—(Exceptional Latinos)
Includes bibliographical references and index.
ISBN 978-0-7660-6716-5 (library binding)
ISBN 978-0-7660-6714-1 (pbk.)
ISBN 978-0-7660-6715-8 (6-pack)
1. Kahlo, Frida—Juvenile literature. 2. Painters—Mexico—Biography—Juvenile literature. I. Title.
ND259.K33 A484 2016
759.972—d23

Printed in the United States of America

Photo Credits: Album/Album/SuperStock, p. 4; AP/ Wide World, pp. 14, 18, 19; David Bank/AWL Images/ Getty Images, p. 7; GDA via AP Images (Frida Kahlo self-portrait), pp. 1, 11; Guillermo Kahlo/Wikimedia Commons/ Frida Kahlo, by Guillermo Kahlo 2.jpg/Public Domain, p. 12; Guillermo Kahlo/Wikimedia Commons/Guillermo Kahlo - Frida Kahlo, June 15, 1919 - Google Art Project. jpg/Public Domain, p. 6; Kgv88/Wikimedia Commons/ File:Celebrations and Ceremonies Totonaca Culture full. jpg/CC BY-SA 3.0, p. 15; Luis Acosta/AFP/Getty Images, p. 21; Toria/Shutterstock.com (blue background).

Cover Credits: GDA via AP Images (Frida Kahlo self-portrait); Toria/Shutterstock.com (blue background).